Recovering from a Breakup
Healing and Moving On

William Pritchard

Published by William Pritchard, 2024.

RECOVERING FROM A BREAKUP HEALING AND MOVING ON

First edition. December 20, 2024.

ISBN: 979-8230237501

Written by William Pritchard.

Also by William Pritchard

Recovering from a Breakup Healing and Moving On
Unplugged How to Find Balance in a Connected World

Table of Contents

Chapter 1: Understanding the Impact of Breakups

Breakups are a universal human experience, yet they often feel intensely personal and isolating. The end of a relationship, whether sudden or gradual, marks a profound shift in your emotional landscape. It's a loss—not just of a person, but of shared dreams, routines, and the sense of identity you built together. To heal, it's crucial to understand the layers of pain and the underlying processes at play.

The Emotional Earthquake

Imagine the emotional equivalent of an earthquake. When a breakup occurs, the foundation you once stood on suddenly shifts, leaving you disoriented and grasping for stability. You might find yourself wondering: Was it my fault? Could I have done something differently? Will I ever feel whole again?

These questions are normal and reflect the universal experience of loss. Here's what you may encounter:

Grief: The absence of your partner creates a void, and it's natural to grieve their presence, even if the relationship had challenges.

Anger: Frustration may emerge, directed at your ex, yourself, or the universe for the perceived injustice.

Confusion: Losing someone you cared for can leave you questioning your value, decisions, and even your future.

Shock: If the breakup was unexpected, you might feel a sense of disbelief or numbness.

Case Study: Take Sarah, for example. When her five-year relationship ended abruptly, she felt a mix of devastation and confusion. She couldn't understand why her partner walked away after years of planning a life together. What Sarah didn't realize then was that her feelings of grief and anger were normal reactions to such a significant loss.

The Science Behind Heartbreak

Breakups aren't just emotionally painful—they're biologically taxing. Neuroscience reveals that your brain experiences a breakup much like withdrawal from an addictive drug. The person you loved became a primary source of dopamine and oxytocin, chemicals associated with pleasure, bonding, and happiness.

Hormonal Havoc

Cortisol Overload: When a relationship ends, your body's stress hormone, cortisol, often spikes. This can lead to sleeplessness, a weakened immune system, and physical fatigue.

Dopamine Deficiency: With your "reward system" disrupted, you might feel unmotivated or emotionally drained.

Oxytocin Withdrawal: Known as the "love hormone," oxytocin fosters connection. Without it, feelings of loneliness can become overwhelming.

Brain Chemistry in Action

Studies using MRI scans have shown that areas of the brain linked to physical pain are activated when someone experiences emotional rejection. This explains why a breakup doesn't just feel like a mental wound—it can manifest as actual physical discomfort.

Debunking Myths About Healing

There's no one-size-fits-all approach to moving on. Society often perpetuates myths that can make you feel like you're failing at recovery:

Myth 1: "Time heals all wounds." Time alone doesn't heal—it's what you do with that time that matters.

Myth 2: "You need to get over it quickly." Healing isn't a race. It's okay if the process takes weeks, months, or even longer.

Myth 3: "Distractions are the best medicine." While staying busy can help, avoiding emotions entirely often prolongs the pain.

Practical Tip: Instead of focusing on societal expectations, honor your unique journey. Healing takes patience and self-compassion.

THE GRIEVING PROCESS

Grieving a breakup is a lot like mourning any significant loss. You've lost not just a person but the version of yourself you were with them and the future you envisioned together. Elisabeth Kübler-Ross's five stages of grief—denial, anger, bargaining, depression, and acceptance—are a useful framework, but it's essential to remember that grief isn't linear.

1. Denial

In the denial stage, you might find yourself holding on to hope that the breakup isn't permanent. Perhaps you believe they'll change their mind or that reconciliation is just around the corner. Denial can act as an emotional buffer, giving you time to process the enormity of the situation.

2. Anger

Anger can be a powerful emotion, but it's often a mask for deeper feelings of hurt and betrayal. You might direct your anger at your ex, yourself, or external circumstances. While anger can feel overwhelming, it's also an essential step toward release.

3. Bargaining

This stage often involves "what if" or "if only" thinking. You may replay moments from the relationship, wishing you had acted differently or hoping that a grand gesture will undo the breakup.

4. Depression

The sadness of a breakup can be profound, especially when the reality of the loss sets in. This stage often feels like the darkest part of the journey, but it's also where healing begins to take root.

5. Acceptance

Acceptance doesn't mean you no longer feel pain—it means you've come to terms with the loss and can begin to move forward.

The Importance of Acknowledging the Pain

Many people try to "move on" by burying their emotions. They throw themselves into work, dive into rebound relationships, or distract themselves with endless activities. While these tactics may offer temporary relief, they often delay true healing.

Give Yourself Permission to Grieve: Healing begins when you allow yourself to feel the full spectrum of emotions.

Avoid the Comparison Trap: Your timeline is your own. Comparing yourself to others will only add unnecessary pressure.

Reflection Exercise: Write a letter to yourself acknowledging your pain. Be honest about your feelings and validate your experiences.

REFRAMING THE BREAKUP as Growth

Though breakups are painful, they can also serve as opportunities for self-discovery and growth. Every ending carries with it the seeds of a new beginning.

What Did You Learn? Reflecting on the relationship can help you identify patterns, understand your needs, and set healthier boundaries in the future.

Focus on Your Strengths: A breakup is a chance to reconnect with the parts of yourself that may have been overlooked during the relationship.

Redefine Your Story: Instead of viewing the breakup as a failure, see it as a chapter in your life that shaped who you are.

Practical Tools for the First Step

Journaling: Write about your emotions, memories, and fears. This can help you process and release pent-up feelings.

Talk It Out: Share your thoughts with a trusted friend or therapist. Verbalizing emotions often brings clarity.

Self-Care Rituals: Treat yourself kindly—whether that's through nourishing meals, long walks, or simply allowing yourself a day to rest.

KEY TAKEAWAYS

Breakups are emotionally and biologically challenging, but they're also a universal part of life.

Allow yourself to grieve and acknowledge the full range of emotions you're experiencing.

Healing takes time, patience, and active self-compassion.

Chapter 2: The Immediate Aftermath: Self-Care and Support

Breakups leave a trail of emotional and practical chaos in their wake. The initial days and weeks after the end of a relationship can feel like survival mode—your mind races, your body aches, and the world feels unsteady. This is the time to prioritize immediate self-care and seek support to help navigate this turbulent period.

The Shock of Separation

In the immediate aftermath, it's normal to feel like your world has been turned upside down. Whether the breakup was sudden or a long time coming, the finality can be overwhelming. You may feel a mix of sadness, anger, and even numbness. It's important to remind yourself that these feelings are temporary, even if they feel all-consuming.

Why It Feels So Intense

A breakup doesn't just sever emotional ties—it disrupts routines, alters your sense of identity, and challenges your plans for the future. The loss is multidimensional, affecting your mental, physical, and social well-being.

What to Focus On: Right now, your job is to stabilize. This isn't the time to figure out the deeper meaning of the breakup; it's about getting through the day with as much grace and self-compassion as possible.

Self-Care: Your First Line of Defense

In times of emotional crisis, self-care becomes a lifeline. It's tempting to neglect your basic needs when sadness and stress take over, but attending to them can make a profound difference in your ability to heal.

1. Sleep: Resting Through the Storm

Breakups can wreak havoc on your sleep. You may find yourself tossing and turning, replaying conversations, or struggling with a racing mind.

Tips for Better Sleep:

Establish a calming bedtime routine—dim the lights, avoid screens, and try relaxation techniques like deep breathing.

Consider natural aids like chamomile tea or lavender essential oil to promote relaxation.

If your thoughts are overwhelming, keep a journal by your bedside to offload them before sleep.

2. Nutrition: Fuel for Healing

Emotional distress often leads to disrupted eating habits. Some people lose their appetite entirely, while others turn to comfort foods for solace.

What to Aim For:

Opt for nutrient-rich meals that support your body's stress response, such as whole grains, leafy greens, and lean proteins.

Stay hydrated; dehydration can exacerbate feelings of fatigue and stress.

Allow yourself small indulgences, but avoid using food as an emotional crutch.

3. Movement: Energizing the Mind and Body

Exercise might be the last thing on your mind, but it's one of the most effective ways to boost your mood and manage stress.

Start Small: Even a 10-minute walk outdoors can release endorphins and clear your mind.

Try Something New: Activities like yoga, dance, or cycling can provide both a physical and emotional release.

The No-Contact Rule: A Crucial Step

In the immediate aftermath of a breakup, staying in contact with your ex can feel tempting. You might want closure, reassurance, or simply the comfort of their presence. However, maintaining contact often prolongs the healing process and prevents you from truly letting go.

Why No Contact Works

Emotional Clarity: Distance helps you process your emotions without the confusion of ongoing interactions.

Breaking the Habit: Love can feel addictive, and no contact is like detoxing from a dependency.

Protecting Your Progress: Every message, call, or meeting can reopen wounds and set you back.

How to Implement It

Block or mute their number and social media accounts temporarily.

Remove reminders of them from your immediate environment—photos, gifts, or shared playlists.

Enlist a friend to hold you accountable if you feel tempted to reach out.

Managing Social Media Triggers

In today's digital age, social media adds a layer of complexity to breakups. Seeing your ex's posts—or even just their name—can feel like ripping off a scab.

What to Avoid

Obsessively checking their profiles or tracking their activity.

Posting cryptic or emotional updates as a way of "indirectly" communicating with them.

Healthy Alternatives

Take a social media detox to focus on yourself.

Curate your feed by following accounts that inspire and uplift you—think motivational quotes, fitness tips, or cute animals.

Use apps or browser extensions to temporarily block their profiles or hide posts related to them.

Building Your Support System

A breakup can leave you feeling isolated, but you don't have to go through it alone. Leaning on your support system—friends, family, or even strangers in similar situations—can provide comfort and perspective.

1. Friends and Family: Your Emotional Anchors

The people closest to you can be invaluable during this time. Don't hesitate to reach out, even if it's just to vent or seek distraction.

Be Honest About Your Needs: Let them know how they can support you, whether it's a listening ear, a hug, or a Netflix binge session.

Avoid Overloading One Person: Spread your emotional needs across different friends or family members to avoid feeling like a burden.

2. Professional Support: Therapy and Counseling

Breakups can bring up deep-seated issues or emotions that feel overwhelming. A therapist or counselor can help you unpack these feelings in a safe, constructive way.

Benefits of Therapy:

Gain tools to manage emotions and navigate grief.

Explore patterns in your relationships to better understand yourself.

Receive validation and encouragement from an impartial professional.

3. Support Groups and Online Communities

Sometimes, connecting with others who've been through similar experiences can provide a unique sense of understanding and solidarity.

Where to Look: Online forums, social media groups, or local meetups focused on relationship recovery.

Caution: While these groups can be helpful, ensure they foster positivity and growth rather than resentment or negativity.

The Dangers of Rebound Relationships

After a breakup, the idea of diving into a new relationship can feel like an appealing distraction. However, rebounds often complicate the healing process rather than alleviate it.

Why Rebounds Rarely Work

Emotional Band-Aid: Using a new relationship to mask your pain prevents you from addressing the root of your feelings.

Unrealistic Expectations: Placing the burden of your happiness on someone new can strain the relationship.

Comparison Trap: You may find yourself comparing your new partner to your ex, which isn't fair to either of you.

What to Do Instead

Focus on rebuilding your relationship with yourself before involving someone else.

Recognize that it's okay to be single and use this time to rediscover who you are outside of a partnership.

Practical Tips for the First Few Weeks

Create a Routine: Structure provides stability during chaotic times. Establish a daily schedule that includes self-care, work, and leisure activities.

Set Small Goals: Whether it's reading a book, completing a puzzle, or cooking a new recipe, small achievements can boost your confidence.

Practice Gratitude: Each day, write down three things you're grateful for. Shifting your focus to positivity can help reframe your perspective.

KEY TAKEAWAYS

The immediate aftermath of a breakup is about survival and self-preservation. Prioritize basic self-care and establish a support system.

The "no contact" rule and managing social media triggers are essential for emotional clarity and progress.

Rebounding into a new relationship may delay your healing—focus on rediscovering yourself first.

Remember, the pain you're feeling now won't last forever. The steps you take today—no matter how small—lay the foundation for a stronger, healthier future.

Chapter 3: Processing Your Emotions: Acknowledging and Accepting

Breakups unleash a storm of emotions that can feel overwhelming, contradictory, and even paralyzing. You might find yourself shifting from anger to sadness to relief within a single afternoon. These feelings, as chaotic as they seem, are all part of the natural healing process. The key to moving forward lies in allowing yourself to feel them fully, rather than burying them or wishing them away.

In this chapter, we'll explore how to navigate the emotional rollercoaster, express your feelings in healthy ways, and cultivate self-compassion during one of life's most challenging transitions.

Understanding the Emotional Rollercoaster

When a relationship ends, it's not just the bond with your partner that's broken. Your expectations, routines, and even your sense of identity may be deeply shaken. It's no wonder that emotions seem to come in waves—sometimes crashing over you, sometimes retreating, leaving you numb.

The Common Emotions You Might Feel

Anger: Directed at your ex, yourself, or even the universe. Anger often masks deeper emotions like hurt or betrayal.

Sadness: A profound sense of loss for the relationship, the person, or the future you imagined together.

Denial: The refusal to accept that the breakup has happened, holding onto the hope of reconciliation.

Guilt: Replaying moments where you feel you could have acted differently, even if the breakup wasn't your fault.

Relief: Especially if the relationship was toxic or fraught with conflict, it's normal to feel a sense of liberation mixed with your grief.

Why It's Okay to Feel Contradictory Emotions

Emotions aren't linear or mutually exclusive. You can feel anger and sadness simultaneously, or relief and guilt in the same breath. Embracing this complexity is a vital part of the healing process. Every emotion serves a purpose—anger can motivate change, sadness allows for release, and relief signals the start of new possibilities.

The Importance of Acknowledging Your Emotions

Suppressing emotions may seem like an attractive option, especially when they feel overwhelming. But unprocessed emotions have a way of resurfacing in unexpected and often destructive ways. Acknowledging your feelings doesn't mean wallowing in them—it means recognizing their presence and allowing them to flow through you.

Why Suppression Doesn't Work

Imagine stuffing your emotions into a metaphorical backpack. Over time, that backpack becomes heavier and harder to carry. Eventually, it bursts open, spilling its contents in unpredictable ways. Suppression can lead to Increased anxiety or depression.

Strained relationships with friends or family.

Physical symptoms like headaches, fatigue, or tension.

Healthy Ways to Acknowledge Your Emotions

Name Your Feelings: Simply identifying your emotions can help you feel more in control. Instead of saying, "I feel awful," try, "I feel sad, betrayed, and anxious."

Accept Without Judgment: Remind yourself that it's okay to feel this way. Emotions are temporary, and they don't define you.

Create Space for Reflection: Set aside time each day to check in with yourself, whether through journaling, meditation, or simply sitting quietly.

Healthy Outlets for Expressing Emotions

Once you've acknowledged your emotions, the next step is to release them in ways that promote healing rather than prolong pain. Everyone processes emotions differently, so it's important to find outlets that resonate with you.

1. Journaling

Writing is one of the most effective ways to process complex emotions. Putting your thoughts on paper can help untangle the mental knots and provide clarity.

Prompts to Get Started:

What am I feeling right now? Why?

What lessons can I take from this breakup?

What am I most grateful for today?

2. Creative Outlets

Art, music, and other forms of creativity offer a powerful way to channel your emotions. You don't have to be a professional—just expressing yourself can be therapeutic.

Ideas to Explore:

Painting or drawing abstract representations of your emotions.

Creating a playlist that mirrors your journey from sadness to empowerment.

Writing poetry or short stories inspired by your experience.

3. Physical Release

Emotions are stored in the body, so movement can be a powerful way to release pent-up feelings.

Options to Try:

High-intensity activities like running or kickboxing to release anger.

Gentle exercises like yoga or tai chi to calm anxiety.

Dancing freely to your favorite music to lift your spirits.

4. Talking It Out

Sometimes, simply verbalizing your feelings can provide relief. Talk to a trusted friend, family member, or therapist who can listen without judgment.

Managing Difficult Emotions

Some emotions may feel so overwhelming that they seem impossible to face. However, with the right strategies, you can navigate even the most challenging feelings.

Mindfulness for Emotional Awareness

Mindfulness is the practice of being fully present in the moment without judgment. It allows you to observe your emotions without becoming consumed by them.

How to Practice:

Sit in a quiet space and close your eyes.

Focus on your breath, noticing each inhale and exhale.

When emotions arise, acknowledge them without trying to change them. For example, "I notice I'm feeling sadness."

Grounding Techniques

Grounding helps bring you back to the present when emotions feel overwhelming.

The 5-4-3-2-1 Technique:

Identify 5 things you can see.

Identify 4 things you can touch.

Identify 3 things you can hear.

Identify 2 things you can smell.

Identify 1 thing you can taste.

Self-Compassion

Be kind to yourself during this process. It's easy to fall into self-blame or harsh criticism, but healing requires patience and gentleness.

Affirmations to Try:

"I am allowed to feel this way."

"I am doing the best I can."

"This pain is temporary, and I will grow from it."

The Role of Therapy

If your emotions feel unmanageable, consider seeking professional help. A therapist can provide tools and guidance to help you navigate the complexities of heartbreak.

Benefits of Therapy

Emotional Validation: A therapist can help you feel heard and understood.

Perspective: They can offer insights into patterns and behaviors you might not have noticed.

Tools for Coping: From cognitive-behavioral techniques to mindfulness exercises, therapy equips you with practical strategies for healing.

EMBRACING SELF-COMPASSION

Breakups often trigger a harsh inner critic that questions your worth or blames you for the relationship's end. Cultivating self-compassion is one of the most powerful ways to counteract this negativity.

What Self-Compassion Looks Like

Mindfulness: Acknowledge your pain without exaggerating or minimizing it.

Common Humanity: Remind yourself that heartbreak is a universal experience—you are not alone.

Self-Kindness: Speak to yourself the way you would comfort a dear friend.

Key Takeaways

Processing emotions is an essential step toward healing. Allow yourself to feel, rather than suppress, the full spectrum of your emotions.

Healthy outlets like journaling, creativity, and mindfulness can help you release emotions constructively.

Self-compassion is a cornerstone of recovery—treat yourself with the kindness and understanding you deserve.

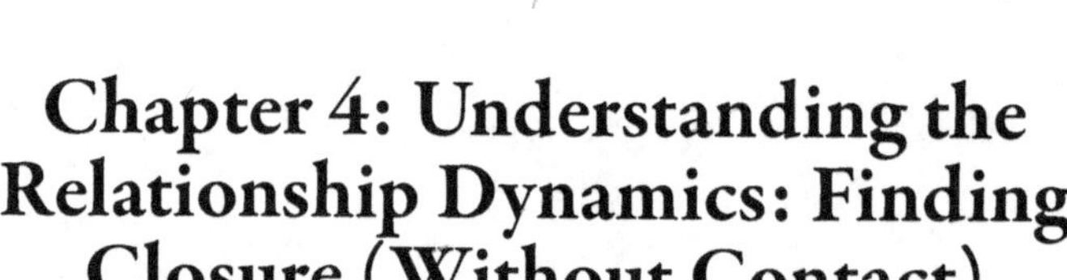

Chapter 4: Understanding the Relationship Dynamics: Finding Closure (Without Contact)

Closure. It's the elusive resolution so many of us crave after a breakup. We want answers, clarity, and a tidy conclusion that ties up loose ends. But here's the uncomfortable truth: closure often doesn't come from external sources. It's something we create within ourselves. In this chapter, we'll explore the dynamics of relationships, unpack patterns and attachment styles, and discover how to find closure without relying on contact with your ex.

The Allure of Closure

After a breakup, it's natural to replay the relationship in your mind, searching for the "why." Why did it end? Why didn't they try harder? Why wasn't I enough? These questions are often at the heart of our longing for closure.

Why We Seek Closure

To Make Sense of the Pain: Breakups feel chaotic, and closure promises order.

To Validate Our Experience: We want acknowledgment that our feelings and efforts mattered.

To Let Go: Closure feels like the final step before we can truly move on.

The Problem with External Closure

While it's tempting to seek closure from your ex, doing so often leads to more confusion than clarity. Even if they offer explanations, they may not align with what you're hoping to hear. True closure comes from within—when you accept the situation as it is and find peace with it.

Understanding the Dynamics of Your Relationship

To create your own closure, it's helpful to reflect on the relationship objectively. What patterns emerged? What lessons can you take away? This process isn't about assigning blame but about gaining insight into your own needs, behaviors, and boundaries.

Attachment Styles and Their Role in Relationships

Attachment theory explains how our early experiences with caregivers influence our patterns of connection in adult relationships. Understanding your attachment style can provide clarity on why certain dynamics played out in your relationship.

Secure Attachment:

Traits: Comfortable with intimacy, trusting, and communicative.

Challenges: If your ex had an insecure attachment style, it might have created tension despite your stability.

Anxious Attachment:

Traits: Craves closeness, fears abandonment, and tends to overanalyze.

Challenges: You may have sought constant reassurance from your partner, leading to dependency or conflict.

Avoidant Attachment:

Traits: Values independence, struggles with vulnerability, and may withdraw emotionally.

Challenges: If your ex had an avoidant style, they might have seemed distant, leaving you feeling neglected.

Fearful-Avoidant Attachment:

Traits: A mix of anxious and avoidant tendencies, often marked by internal conflict.

Challenges: This style can create a push-pull dynamic that's emotionally exhausting.

Reflection Exercise:

Identify your attachment style and your ex's (if possible).

Consider how these styles influenced your communication, conflicts, and emotional connection.

Reflect on what worked and what didn't, focusing on patterns rather than assigning blame.

Identifying Unhealthy Patterns

Every relationship has its ups and downs, but some patterns are particularly destructive. Recognizing these dynamics can help you understand what to avoid in the future.

Common Unhealthy Patterns:

Codependency: When one partner's identity or self-worth becomes overly tied to the other.

Communication Breakdown: Frequent misunderstandings, unresolved conflicts, or avoidance of tough conversations.

Power Imbalances: One partner dominating decisions or controlling aspects of the relationship.

Emotional Neglect: A lack of empathy, support, or validation.

Learning from the Past

Instead of focusing on what went wrong, shift your perspective to what you can learn:

What did the relationship teach you about your needs and boundaries?

What behaviors or patterns would you like to change in the future?

What positive traits or habits would you like to carry forward?

The Danger of Seeking Closure from Your Ex

Reaching out to your ex for answers might seem like the easiest way to find closure, but it often backfires. Even well-intentioned conversations can stir up unresolved emotions, reignite old conflicts, or create false hope.

Why Closure Conversations Often Fail

Different Perspectives: You and your ex may have very different interpretations of the relationship and its end.

Unintended Hurt: They might say something that feels dismissive or invalidating, deepening your pain.

Reopening Wounds: Revisiting the relationship can make it harder to let go.

THE CASE FOR INTERNAL Closure

By focusing on your own thoughts and feelings, you regain control over your healing process. Internal closure is empowering because it doesn't rely on anyone else's input or actions.

Steps to Find Closure Without Contact

Creating closure is a personal and reflective process. It's about finding peace with what happened and focusing on the lessons rather than the loss.

1. Accept the Breakup as It Is

Acceptance doesn't mean you're happy about the breakup—it means you've stopped resisting the reality of it.

Mantra to Repeat: "I can't change the past, but I can shape my future."

Practice Letting Go: When thoughts of "what if" or "if only" arise, acknowledge them and gently redirect your focus to the present.

2. Write a Letter You Don't Send

This exercise allows you to express everything you wish you could say to your ex without the risks of actual communication.

What to Include:

Your feelings about the breakup.

The things you're grateful for from the relationship.

The things you're ready to release.

3. Reframe the Relationship

Instead of viewing the breakup as a failure, consider it a chapter in your life that helped you grow.

Reflection Prompts:

What did I gain from this relationship (e.g., memories, lessons, strengths)?

How has this experience shaped the person I'm becoming?

4. Create a Ritual for Closure

Marking the end of the relationship with a symbolic act can help you move forward.

Ideas for Rituals:

Write down your feelings on paper and burn or bury them as a sign of release.

Create a small memory box with tokens from the relationship, then put it away to symbolize moving on.

Take a meaningful walk in nature, focusing on the idea of letting go with each step.

THE ROLE OF FORGIVENESS in Closure

Forgiveness is a powerful tool for closure—not for your ex, but for yourself. Holding onto resentment or anger only prolongs your pain. Forgiveness doesn't mean excusing harmful behavior; it means releasing its hold on you.

Steps to Forgiveness:

Acknowledge Your Feelings: Allow yourself to feel anger or hurt without judgment.

Shift Your Perspective: Recognize that everyone is flawed and capable of mistakes.

Focus on Your Freedom: Forgiving is about freeing yourself, not condoning their actions.

The Future Beyond Closure

Closure isn't a one-time event—it's a process that unfolds as you grow, reflect, and heal. Over time, the relationship will occupy a smaller and smaller space in your mind, leaving room for new experiences, relationships, and joys.

Key Takeaways

Closure is a personal process that comes from within, not from external sources.

Reflecting on relationship dynamics and patterns helps you gain clarity and insights for the future.

Forgiveness and acceptance are essential steps toward finding peace and moving forward

Chapter 5: Rebuilding Your Self-Esteem and Confidence

A breakup can feel like an earthquake to your sense of self. The person you once shared your life with often plays a role in shaping how you view yourself, and when that connection is severed, self-esteem can take a hit. But here's the good news: rebuilding your confidence isn't just possible—it's transformative. This chapter is about rediscovering your self-worth, rekindling your passions, and embracing the vibrant, confident person you are.

The Self-Esteem Shakedown

When a relationship ends, it's common to question yourself. Thoughts like Was I not enough?, Did I fail?, or Will anyone ever love me again? can haunt even the most secure people. These feelings, while natural, often stem from the emotional fallout of a breakup rather than an accurate reflection of your worth.

Why Breakups Affect Self-Esteem

Shared Identity Loss: In relationships, we often tie our identity to the role we play—partner, supporter, or nurturer. Losing that role can make us feel untethered.

Rejection's Sting: Even if the breakup was mutual, rejection (real or perceived) can bruise your ego.

Comparison Trap:

You may find yourself comparing your life to your ex's—or worse, their new partner's—through the distorted lens of social media.

The Key Realization

Your worth isn't defined by another person's ability to see it. It existed before your relationship and remains intact, even if it feels temporarily buried.

Step 1: Reframe Your Inner Dialogue

The way you talk to yourself has a profound impact on your confidence. After a breakup, it's easy to fall into the trap of self-criticism, replaying what you think you "did wrong." It's time to rewrite that narrative.

Identify Negative Self-Talk

Pay attention to the phrases you say to yourself, like:

"I'll never find love again."

"I wasn't good enough."

"I wasted so much time."

Flip the Script

Challenge these thoughts by replacing them with affirmations rooted in truth and self-compassion:

"I am worthy of love and happiness."

"This relationship taught me valuable lessons."

"I'm growing and evolving every day."

Practical Exercise

Write down three negative thoughts you've had about yourself since the breakup. Then, reframe each one into a positive or neutral statement. Repeat these affirmations daily to train your brain to focus on your strengths.

Step 2: Rediscover Your Passions

Breakups often free up time and energy that were previously devoted to your relationship. This is the perfect opportunity to reconnect with activities, hobbies, and goals that make you feel alive.

Why Passions Matter

Boosting Self-Worth: Pursuing your interests reminds you of your unique talents and abilities.

Creating Joy: Engaging in activities you love naturally elevates your mood.

Building Independence: Hobbies are a great way to reconnect with your identity outside of a relationship.

Ideas to Explore

Revisit old hobbies: Was there a skill or activity you loved before the relationship? Dust it off and give it another go.

Try something new: Whether it's pottery, rock climbing, or learning a language, stepping out of your comfort zone builds confidence.

Create something: Painting, writing, or crafting can be therapeutic and empowering.

Case Study: After her breakup, Emily decided to join a local hiking group. Not only did it reignite her love for nature, but it also introduced her to new friends who shared her enthusiasm. Each hike reminded her of her strength and resilience.

Step 3: Celebrate Small Wins

Rebuilding confidence doesn't happen overnight. It's a gradual process of setting small goals and achieving them, one step at a time. Each win, no matter how minor, reinforces your belief in your capabilities.

Set Achievable Goals

Start with manageable tasks that push you slightly out of your comfort zone:

Social: Attend a gathering or meet a friend for coffee.

Personal: Cook a new recipe or complete a workout routine.

Professional: Update your resume or tackle a project at work.

Track Your Progress

Keep a journal or use a habit tracker to document your achievements. Seeing your progress on paper can be incredibly motivating.

Reward Yourself

Celebrate your wins, big or small. Treat yourself to something you enjoy, like a favorite meal, a new book, or a relaxing bath.

Step 4: Prioritize Self-Love

Self-love isn't just a buzzword—it's a cornerstone of confidence. When you treat yourself with the same kindness and care you'd offer a loved one, you begin to rebuild a solid foundation of self-worth.

Daily Self-Love Practices

Start the Day with Gratitude: Each morning, list three things you appreciate about yourself or your life.

Practice Mindful Grooming: Take the time to care for your appearance—not to impress others, but to feel good about yourself.

Invest in Rest: Sleep is a vital part of emotional resilience. Create a bedtime routine that promotes relaxation and rejuvenation.

Create a Self-Love Ritual

Dedicate a specific time each week to something that brings you joy, like a solo movie night, a relaxing spa day, or a walk in nature. This ritual reinforces the idea that you're worth prioritizing.

STEP 5: BUILD POSITIVE Connections

While self-esteem comes from within, surrounding yourself with supportive people can amplify your efforts. Healthy relationships remind you of your value and offer encouragement as you rebuild.

Lean on Your Support System

Reach out to friends and family who uplift you. Share your thoughts and experiences, and allow them to remind you of your strengths.

Expand Your Circle

Consider joining a club, class, or group to meet like-minded individuals. New connections can help you rediscover parts of yourself you may have neglected during your relationship.

Step 6: Reflect on Your Strengths

Breakups have a way of making us focus on what went wrong, but it's equally important to acknowledge what you did right. Reflecting on your strengths helps you shift from self-doubt to self-confidence.

Reflection Prompts

What challenges have I overcome in the past, and how did I handle them?

What qualities or traits make me a good friend, partner, or person?

What have I achieved in my personal or professional life that I'm proud of?

Exercise: Write a "confidence resume" highlighting your accomplishments, skills, and positive traits. Refer to it whenever self-doubt creeps in.

Step 7: Embrace Your Independence

Rediscovering your independence after a breakup can feel daunting, but it's also incredibly empowering. Being single isn't just a relationship status—it's a chance to focus entirely on your growth and happiness.

Reframe Singlehood

Instead of thinking, "I'm alone," think, "I have the freedom to explore who I am."

Use this time to focus on your goals, interests, and self-improvement.

Take Yourself on Dates

Spend quality time with yourself. Whether it's visiting a museum, going to the cinema, or enjoying a meal out, these solo adventures reinforce that your own company is enough.

Key Takeaways

Breakups may shake your self-esteem, but they don't define your worth.

Rebuilding confidence starts with small, consistent steps, like reframing your inner dialogue and celebrating wins.

Rediscovering your passions, embracing independence, and prioritizing self-love can transform this challenging period into a time of growth and empowerment.

Chapter 6: Letting Go of the Past: Forgiveness and Acceptance

Breakups often leave behind an emotional residue—anger, resentment, sadness, or even guilt. These lingering feelings can act like chains, tethering you to a relationship that no longer serves you. Letting go of the past doesn't mean erasing the memories or excusing hurtful behavior; it means freeing yourself from the emotional weight that keeps you stuck. In this chapter, we'll explore how to release negative emotions, embrace forgiveness, and move toward acceptance.

The Emotional Weight of Holding On

Imagine carrying a heavy backpack everywhere you go. The contents of the bag—resentment, regret, and unresolved feelings—wear you down over time, sapping your energy and joy. Holding onto the pain of a breakup can have a similar effect, preventing you from moving forward and fully embracing the present.

Why It's Hard to Let Go

The Need for Justice: You might feel that holding onto anger keeps the scales balanced, especially if your ex wronged you.

Fear of Forgetting: Letting go can feel like diminishing the importance of the relationship or the lessons it taught you.

Attachment to the "What Ifs": Ruminating on how things could have been different can make it harder to accept what is.

The Truth About Letting Go

Letting go isn't about forgetting or dismissing the past—it's about choosing to focus on your own well-being. It's an act of self-love, not a favor to your ex.

Step 1: Acknowledge Your Feelings

Before you can let go, you need to face your emotions head-on. Suppressing anger, sadness, or regret only pushes them deeper, where they can manifest as anxiety, depression, or bitterness.

Allow Yourself to Feel

Journaling Exercise: Write a letter to yourself or your ex (without sending it) to express your feelings fully. Be honest about your hurt, anger, or disappointment.

Emotional Awareness: When a wave of emotion hits, pause and identify what you're feeling. Naming emotions can reduce their intensity and help you process them.

Avoid Toxic Positivity

It's okay to admit that you're struggling. Telling yourself to "just move on" before you've processed your feelings can create additional pressure and guilt.

Step 2: Understand the Role of Forgiveness

Forgiveness is often misunderstood. It's not about condoning bad behavior or letting someone off the hook; it's about freeing yourself from the grip of negative emotions. When you forgive, you reclaim your power and shift your focus from the past to the present.

Who Do You Need to Forgive?

Your Ex: Forgiving your ex doesn't mean rekindling the relationship. It means releasing the anger and hurt that bind you to them.

Yourself: Self-forgiveness is just as important. It's easy to blame yourself for the breakup or dwell on perceived mistakes, but holding onto guilt only prolongs the healing process.

Benefits of Forgiveness

Reduces stress and anxiety.

Improves emotional and physical health.

Creates space for joy and new experiences.

Step 3: Practice Techniques for Letting Go

Letting go is an active process. It requires intention, effort, and patience. Here are some techniques to help you release the past and move forward.

1. Mindfulness Meditation

Mindfulness teaches you to focus on the present moment rather than ruminating on the past or worrying about the future.

How to Start:

Find a quiet space and sit comfortably.

Close your eyes and focus on your breath.

When thoughts about your ex arise, acknowledge them without judgment and gently bring your attention back to your breath.

2. Visualization Exercise

Visualizing yourself letting go of the past can be a powerful tool.

Try This:

Imagine holding a balloon filled with your negative emotions.

Picture yourself releasing the balloon into the sky, watching it drift further away until it disappears.

3. Rituals of Release

Symbolic acts can provide closure and help you let go emotionally.

Examples:

Write down your feelings and burn the paper as a way of releasing them.

Create a memory box with items from the relationship, then store it away or donate the items.

4. Gratitude Journaling

Shifting your focus from what you've lost to what you're grateful for can help reframe your mindset.

Prompts:

What lessons did the relationship teach me?

What strengths have I discovered in myself since the breakup?

What aspects of my life bring me joy right now?

Step 4: Embrace Acceptance

Acceptance is the final and most liberating step in letting go. It doesn't mean you're happy about the breakup or that you no longer feel sadness. It means you've come to terms with what happened and are ready to move forward.

What Acceptance Looks Like

You no longer feel the need to replay or analyze the breakup.

Thoughts of your ex don't provoke strong emotional reactions.

You're focused on your future rather than your past.

How to Cultivate Acceptance

Stop Seeking Closure from Your Ex: Closure comes from within, not from external validation.

Reframe the Breakup: Instead of viewing it as a failure, see it as a chapter that shaped your growth.

Celebrate Your Progress: Acknowledge the small steps you've taken toward healing, even if you're not fully there yet.

Step 5: Focus on the Present and Future

Letting go of the past allows you to fully embrace the present and look forward to the future. This is your opportunity to rebuild, rediscover, and redefine yourself.

Set New Goals

Personal: Pursue hobbies, learn a new skill, or focus on self-care.

Professional: Take on new challenges or explore career opportunities.

Social: Strengthen existing relationships or make new connections.

VISUALIZE YOUR FUTURE

Spend time imagining the life you want to create. What does happiness look like for you? What steps can you take to get there?

Key Takeaways

Letting go of the past is an act of self-love that frees you from emotional burdens.

Forgiveness isn't about excusing behavior—it's about reclaiming your peace.

Acceptance is the foundation for moving forward and embracing new possibilities.

The process of letting go may feel daunting, but it's also a transformative journey. Each step you take—no matter how small—brings you closer to the freedom and happiness you deserve.

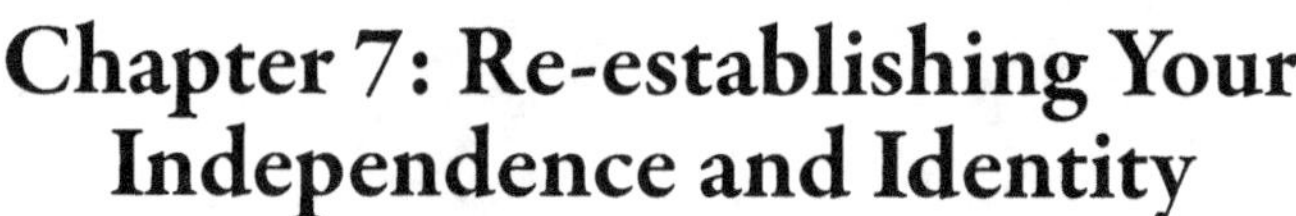

Chapter 7: Re-establishing Your Independence and Identity

A breakup often leaves a void where shared routines, plans, and even your sense of identity once thrived. When a relationship ends, it's natural to feel untethered—wondering who you are without your partner. Rebuilding your independence is not just about reclaiming your life; it's about rediscovering your strength, passions, and identity. This chapter focuses on helping you rebuild from the inside out, empowering you to stand tall as your most authentic self.

The Identity Crisis After a Breakup

When you're part of a couple, it's easy for your identity to merge with your partner's. You might have made choices together, adopted their habits, or shifted your own priorities to align with theirs. While this interdependence is natural, it can also leave you feeling lost after the relationship ends.

Why Breakups Shake Your Sense of Self

Shared Identity Loss: Your routines, hobbies, or even social circles may have revolved around your partner.

The Questioning Phase: You might find yourself questioning your own likes, dislikes, and goals—were they truly yours, or influenced by the relationship?

Fear of the Unknown: Being single can feel like uncharted territory, especially if it's been a while since you navigated life on your own.

Step 1: Embrace Being Alone

The thought of being alone can be daunting, but it's also an incredible opportunity for growth. Solitude allows you to reconnect with yourself and discover who you are outside the context of a relationship.

Learn to Enjoy Your Own Company

Start Small: Dedicate a few minutes each day to doing something you enjoy by yourself, like reading, meditating, or taking a walk.

Take Yourself on Dates: Visit a museum, enjoy a solo dinner, or see a movie you've been curious about. Celebrate the freedom to choose exactly what you want to do.

Reframe Loneliness as Freedom

Instead of seeing your newfound independence as loneliness, view it as an opportunity to make decisions without compromise. This is your time to focus entirely on your own happiness.

Step 2: Redefine Your Routines

When a relationship ends, your daily life can feel disrupted. Re-establishing routines that align with your own preferences and goals is a powerful way to regain stability.

Assess Your Current Routine

What's Missing? Identify gaps in your routine that were once filled by your partner. These might include weekend plans, shared meals, or conversations.

What Do You Want to Add? Think about habits or activities you've always wanted to incorporate but didn't prioritize during the relationship.

Build a New Structure

Morning Rituals: Start your day with an activity that energizes you, like yoga, journaling, or a nutritious breakfast.

Evening Wind-Down: Create a calming nighttime routine that helps you relax and reflect on your day.

Weekly Adventures: Plan one new experience each week—whether it's trying a new restaurant, exploring a park, or taking a class.

Step 3: Reconnect with Old Passions

Breakups provide a unique opportunity to revisit hobbies or interests that may have taken a backseat during the relationship. Rekindling your passions can reignite your sense of purpose and joy.

Reflect on Your Pre-Relationship Self

What Did You Love? Think back to the activities, interests, or goals that brought you happiness before your relationship.

What Have You Always Wanted to Try? Use this time to explore new hobbies or revisit ones you've set aside.

Dive In Wholeheartedly

Join a club or class to meet others who share your interests.

Dedicate time each week to pursuing your hobbies, whether it's painting, gardening, or playing a sport.

Set a goal related to your passion, like completing a project or participating in an event.

Example: After his breakup, Tom rediscovered his love for photography. He started taking weekend trips to capture landscapes, which not only gave him a creative outlet but also helped him reconnect with nature and himself.

Step 4: Set Personal Goals

Breakups often leave a sense of unfinished business. Setting personal goals can help you regain a sense of direction and accomplishment.

START WITH SMALL, ACHIEVABLE Goals

Health: Commit to exercising three times a week or cooking more meals at home.

Career: Take a professional development course or update your resume.

Creative: Write a short story, complete a puzzle, or learn to play an instrument.

Create a Vision Board

Visualizing your goals can make them feel more tangible. Use a corkboard or digital platform to display images, quotes, and milestones that inspire you.

Step 5: Strengthen Your Social Connections

Re-establishing independence doesn't mean isolating yourself. Friends and family can be invaluable sources of support, encouragement, and companionship as you navigate this new chapter.

Reconnect with Your Support System

Check In: Reach out to friends or family members you may have drifted from during your relationship.

Plan Gatherings: Host a dinner, movie night, or outing to rebuild bonds and create new memories.

Lean on Trusted Allies: Share your thoughts and feelings with people who uplift and support you.

Expand Your Social Circle

Join Groups or Clubs: Meet like-minded individuals by participating in community activities or online forums.

Volunteer: Giving back can be a fulfilling way to connect with others while contributing to a cause you care about.

Be Open to New Friendships: You never know who might enter your life when you're open to new experiences.

Step 6: Establish Healthy Boundaries

Rebuilding independence also means setting boundaries that protect your well-being. This includes boundaries with your ex, friends, and even yourself.

Boundary Tips:

With Your Ex: Limit or avoid contact to give yourself space to heal.

With Others: Politely decline invitations or conversations that feel draining or overwhelming.

With Yourself: Resist the urge to dwell on the past or engage in negative self-talk.

Step 7: Celebrate Your Growth

As you rebuild your independence and identity, take time to acknowledge your progress. Each step you take—no matter how small—is a testament to your resilience and strength.

Document Your Journey

Keep a journal to track your thoughts, achievements, and lessons learned.

Take photos or create a scrapbook of experiences that symbolize your journey toward independence.

Reward Yourself

Celebrate milestones, whether it's completing a project, making a new friend, or simply feeling more confident in your own skin. Treat yourself to something special—a day trip, a spa day, or a new book.

Key Takeaways

Re-establishing independence after a breakup is a chance to rediscover your identity, passions, and goals.

Embrace solitude as an opportunity for self-reflection and growth.

Build new routines, reconnect with old passions, and strengthen your social connections.

Celebrate your progress and remember that rebuilding your life is a journey, not a race.

This chapter is about reclaiming your sense of self and creating a life that reflects who you are at your core. With every step you take, you're not just moving on—you're moving toward a brighter, more fulfilling future.

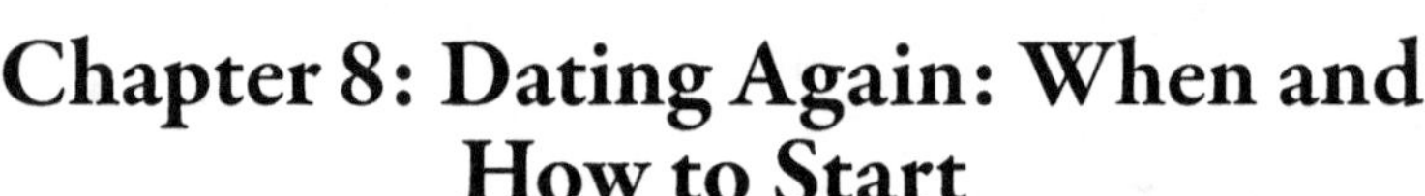

Chapter 8: Dating Again: When and How to Start

The idea of dating after a breakup can feel like a mixed bag of excitement, dread, and uncertainty. For some, it might seem too soon; for others, the thought of re-entering the dating world brings a spark of hope. Wherever you fall on this spectrum, deciding when and how to start dating again is a deeply personal choice. In this chapter, we'll explore the signs that you're ready, practical tips for navigating the dating world, and how to approach new relationships with a healthy mindset.

Are You Ready to Date Again?

Dating too soon after a breakup can feel like jumping into deep waters before you've learned to swim again. While there's no universal timeline, there are emotional benchmarks that can help you determine whether you're ready to put yourself out there.

Signs You're Ready

You Feel Stable on Your Own: You're comfortable with your independence and don't feel desperate for companionship.

Your Ex Is No Longer Front and Center: Thoughts of your ex no longer dominate your day, and you're not using dating as a way to distract yourself from lingering emotions.

You Know What You Want: You have clarity about the qualities and values you're looking for in a partner and are ready to approach dating with intention.

Signs You Might Not Be Ready

You're Still Comparing Everyone to Your Ex: It's natural to compare initially, but if you're constantly holding others to the standard of your past relationship, it may be too soon.

You're Seeking Validation: If you're dating to feel attractive, worthy, or lovable, it's a sign to focus on building self-esteem first.

The Idea of Rejection Feels Devastating: While rejection is never pleasant, it shouldn't completely unravel your sense of self.

The No-Pressure Approach to Dating

Re-entering the dating world doesn't have to be an all-or-nothing endeavor. Think of it as dipping your toes into the water rather than diving in headfirst.

Start Slowly

Casual Conversations: Begin with low-pressure interactions, like chatting with someone at a coffee shop or joining a group activity.

Practice Being Present: Focus on enjoying the moment rather than worrying about whether this person is "The One."

SET REALISTIC EXPECTATIONS

Dating isn't a guaranteed path to finding a new relationship—it's a process of meeting people, exploring connections, and learning about yourself.

Experiment Without Commitment

Try different ways of meeting people, from online dating to social events.

Use these experiences to gauge what you're looking for and how you feel about being in the dating world again.

How to Meet People in Today's World

The dating landscape has changed dramatically in recent years, with technology playing a significant role. Whether you're tech-savvy or prefer a more traditional approach, there are plenty of options to explore.

1. Online Dating

Online dating is one of the most popular ways to meet people, but it comes with its own set of rules and challenges.

Tips for Success:

Be honest in your profile—authenticity attracts genuine connections.

Use recent photos that represent who you are today.

Set boundaries for how much time you spend swiping or chatting to avoid burnout.

Popular Platforms:

Bumble: Women initiate the conversation, which can create a safer environment.

Hinge: Focused on meaningful connections, with prompts to spark conversation.

Tinder: Great for casual dating or exploring what's out there.

2. Social Activities and Hobbies

Joining groups, classes, or clubs is a natural way to meet people who share your interests.

Examples:

Take a cooking or art class.

Join a hiking group or sports team.

Volunteer for a cause you're passionate about.

3. Through Friends and Family

Let your loved ones know you're open to meeting new people. They might have someone in mind who could be a great match.

Setting Healthy Boundaries

One of the most important aspects of dating after a breakup is maintaining healthy boundaries—both with others and yourself.

Emotional Boundaries

Be clear about your intentions. Are you looking for something casual, a serious relationship, or just companionship?

Take things slow. Avoid rushing into emotional intimacy before you feel ready.

Physical Boundaries

Only move at a pace that feels comfortable for you. If someone pressures you, they're not respecting your boundaries.

Communicate openly about your comfort levels.

Time Boundaries

Balance dating with other aspects of your life, like work, hobbies, and friendships.

Avoid making someone new the center of your world too soon.

Recognizing Red Flags

Dating again is a learning process, and part of that process involves recognizing signs that someone may not be a good match for you.

Common Red Flags

Inconsistent Communication: They disappear for days, only to reappear with vague explanations.

Lack of Respect for Boundaries: They pressure you to move faster than you're comfortable with.

Excessive Negativity: They constantly complain or badmouth their ex, signaling unresolved issues.

Too Much, Too Soon: They push for serious commitment early on without giving the relationship time to grow.

Trust Your Gut

If something feels off, don't ignore it. Your instincts are a valuable guide in navigating new relationships.

Approaching New Relationships with a Healthy Mindset

When you do find someone you connect with, it's important to approach the relationship with the lessons you've learned from your past. This ensures you're building something strong and healthy.

1. Communicate Clearly

Share your intentions early to ensure you're on the same page.

Practice active listening, showing genuine interest in their thoughts and feelings.

2. Maintain Your Independence

Continue pursuing your own goals, hobbies, and friendships.

Avoid losing yourself in the relationship; balance is key.

3. Be Open to Vulnerability

Allow yourself to be seen and known, but don't feel pressured to share everything at once.

Understand that vulnerability is a sign of strength, not weakness.

4. Learn From Past Mistakes

Reflect on patterns or behaviors that didn't serve you in your previous relationship.

Work to build trust, respect, and healthy communication from the start.

When Things Don't Work Out

Not every connection will lead to a lasting relationship, and that's okay. Each experience is a stepping stone toward understanding yourself and what you want.

How to Handle Rejection

Don't take it personally. Rejection often says more about the other person's needs than your worth.

Reflect on the experience. What did you learn about yourself or what you want in a partner?

Moving Forward

Remind yourself that dating is a journey, not a race.

Keep an open mind and heart as you continue exploring new connections.

Key Takeaways

There's no rush to start dating again—take your time and assess your readiness.

Approach dating with curiosity and self-awareness, rather than pressure or expectation.

Maintain healthy boundaries and learn to recognize red flags early.

Every experience, whether positive or negative, helps you grow and move closer to finding the right connection.

Dating again after a breakup is a brave step toward opening your heart to new possibilities. With patience, self-awareness, and a touch of optimism, this chapter of your life can be as rewarding as it is transformative.

Chapter 9: Building Healthy Future Relationships

After navigating the emotional maze of a breakup and rediscovering yourself, stepping into a new relationship can feel both exciting and daunting. While past experiences may influence your approach to love, they also provide valuable lessons about what works, what doesn't, and what you truly need from a partner. This chapter explores how to apply those lessons, nurture healthy relationship dynamics, and build a partnership grounded in trust, respect, and shared values.

Learning from the Past

Every relationship, regardless of how it ended, holds valuable insights. Reflecting on your past relationships can help you identify patterns, recognize areas for growth, and clarify your needs.

Reflection Exercise:

What Worked? Consider the positive aspects of your past relationships—qualities you valued in your partner, moments that brought you joy, and dynamics that felt healthy.

What Didn't Work? Identify behaviors, conflicts, or patterns that led to tension or unhappiness.

What Have You Learned About Yourself? Reflect on how you showed up in your relationships. Did you communicate effectively? Did you set boundaries?

By taking the time to analyze these aspects, you can approach future relationships with greater self-awareness and intention.

The Foundations of a Healthy Relationship

Building a healthy relationship requires more than just chemistry or compatibility. It involves mutual respect, effective communication, and a shared commitment to growth.

Key Ingredients of Healthy Relationships

Trust: The cornerstone of any strong partnership. Trust is built through consistency, honesty, and vulnerability.

Respect: Valuing each other's individuality, boundaries, and perspectives.

Communication: Open and honest dialogue about needs, feelings, and concerns.

Shared Values: Aligning on important aspects like goals, family, and lifestyle.

Independence: Maintaining your own identity and interests outside the relationship.

Practical Tips for Building These Foundations

Take the time to get to know your partner's values, habits, and aspirations.

Create an environment where both of you feel safe to express yourselves without fear of judgment.

Celebrate each other's achievements and provide support during challenges.

Understanding Attachment Styles

Your attachment style, shaped by early experiences, influences how you connect with others in romantic relationships. Understanding your own style—and your partner's—can help you navigate challenges and deepen your connection.

The Four Attachment Styles

Secure: Comfortable with intimacy and independence.

Anxious: Craves closeness and fears abandonment.

Avoidant: Values independence and struggles with vulnerability.

Fearful-Avoidant: A mix of anxious and avoidant tendencies.

How to Use This Knowledge

If You're Secure: Leverage your natural strengths in communication and trust to support your partner.

If You're Anxious or Avoidant: Work on self-awareness and emotional regulation. Therapy or self-help resources can be incredibly beneficial.

If Your Partner Has a Different Style: Approach differences with empathy and patience, recognizing that growth is a shared journey.

Setting Healthy Boundaries

Boundaries aren't about keeping people out—they're about creating space for mutual respect and understanding. Setting boundaries early in a relationship helps prevent misunderstandings and fosters a sense of security.

Common Relationship Boundaries

Time: Balancing time together with time apart to nurture individual interests.

Communication: Agreeing on how to handle conflicts or sensitive topics.

Physical Intimacy: Discussing comfort levels and expectations.

Personal Space: Respecting each other's need for solitude or privacy.

How to Communicate Boundaries

Use "I" statements to express your needs (e.g., "I feel overwhelmed when...").

Be clear and direct, avoiding vague language.

Revisit boundaries periodically as the relationship evolves.

Red Flags to Watch For

While it's important to focus on building a healthy relationship, it's equally crucial to recognize signs that a partnership may not be in your best interest.

Common Red Flags

Controlling Behavior: Attempts to dictate your actions, choices, or relationships.

Lack of Respect: Dismissing your feelings, opinions, or boundaries.

Emotional Unavailability: Difficulty opening up or committing to the relationship.

Excessive Jealousy: Constant suspicion or attempts to isolate you from others.

Inconsistent Effort: Hot-and-cold behavior that leaves you feeling uncertain.

What to Do If You Spot Red Flags

Trust your instincts. If something feels off, don't ignore it.

Communicate your concerns and observe their response. A healthy partner will listen and strive to address the issue.

Be prepared to walk away if the relationship doesn't align with your needs and values.

Fostering Emotional Intimacy

Emotional intimacy is the glue that binds relationships together. It's about feeling deeply connected to your partner on an emotional level, beyond physical attraction or shared activities.

Ways to Build Emotional Intimacy

Share Vulnerabilities: Open up about your fears, dreams, and past experiences.

Practice Active Listening: Show genuine interest in your partner's thoughts and feelings.

Create Rituals Together: Whether it's a weekly date night or a morning coffee routine, shared rituals strengthen your bond.

Express Appreciation: Regularly acknowledge what you value about your partner.

Healing Together

Even in healthy relationships, challenges and conflicts are inevitable. What sets strong partnerships apart is the ability to navigate these moments together.

Conflict Resolution Tips

Focus on the Issue: Avoid bringing up unrelated grievances during an argument.

Use "I" Statements: Express how you feel without assigning blame (e.g., "I feel hurt when...").

Take Breaks if Needed: If emotions run high, step away to cool down before continuing the conversation.

Collaborate on Solutions: Approach conflicts as a team, working together to find resolutions.

Cultivating Long-Term Growth

Healthy relationships aren't static—they evolve over time. By fostering a growth mindset, you can navigate life's changes while maintaining a strong connection.

Ways to Grow Together

Set Shared Goals: Discuss your aspirations as a couple, whether it's traveling, starting a family, or supporting each other's careers.

Encourage Individual Growth: Support each other's personal goals and celebrate achievements.

Practice Gratitude: Regularly reflect on what you're grateful for in your relationship.

Balancing Love and Independence

One of the keys to a thriving partnership is maintaining a balance between closeness and individuality. Healthy relationships allow both partners to grow together while retaining their unique identities.

Tips for Maintaining Balance

Make time for your own hobbies, friendships, and self-care.

Encourage your partner to do the same.

Avoid codependency by fostering mutual respect and trust.

Key Takeaways

Apply lessons from past relationships to build stronger, healthier connections in the future.

Focus on trust, respect, communication, and shared values as the foundation of a healthy relationship.

Set boundaries and recognize red flags to protect your emotional well-being.

Cultivate emotional intimacy and a growth mindset to create a partnership that stands the test of time.

Building a healthy future relationship isn't about perfection—it's about progress. By approaching love with self-awareness, openness, and intention, you can create a connection that brings out the best in both you and your partner.

Chapter 10: Moving Forward: Embracing the Future

Breakups are undeniably tough, but they're also a turning point—a chance to rewrite your story and embrace new beginnings. The end of one chapter doesn't mean the end of the book; it's an opportunity to start fresh, equipped with the lessons you've learned and the resilience you've gained. In this chapter, we'll focus on how to move forward, rediscover joy, and embrace the possibilities that lie ahead.

The Power of Perspective

Moving forward starts with shifting your mindset. While it's easy to dwell on what was lost, focusing on what lies ahead can transform pain into possibility.

From Setback to Opportunity

Reframe the Breakup: Instead of seeing it as a failure, view it as a stepping stone to personal growth.

Acknowledge Your Strength: Surviving heartbreak proves your resilience. Celebrate the fact that you're still standing.

Look for Silver Linings: What doors has this breakup opened? Perhaps it's a chance to pursue goals, rediscover passions, or meet new people.

Journal Prompt:

Write a letter to your future self, describing the life you envision a year from now. Include the goals you've achieved, the happiness you've found, and the ways you've grown.

Step 1: Rediscover Your Joy

Breakups can cast a shadow over your life, making it easy to forget what happiness feels like. Rediscovering joy is about finding small moments of light and allowing them to grow.

Start Small

Daily Gratitude: Write down three things you're grateful for each day, no matter how small.

Indulge in Simple Pleasures: Enjoy a cup of tea, watch a sunset, or listen to your favorite music.

Reconnect with Your Passions

Explore hobbies you once loved or try something entirely new.

Engage in activities that make you lose track of time, whether it's painting, dancing, or gardening.

Example: After her breakup, Sarah signed up for a pottery class. Not only did it give her a creative outlet, but it also became a source of joy and a way to meet new friends.

Step 2: Set New Life Goals

Breakups often disrupt plans and dreams you shared with your partner. While this can feel disorienting, it's also a chance to create a vision for your future that's entirely your own.

Define Your Goals

Short-Term: Focus on immediate steps, like improving your fitness, learning a skill, or redecorating your space.

Long-Term: Envision where you want to be in 5 or 10 years. This might include career aspirations, travel plans, or personal growth milestones.

Create an Action Plan

Break your goals into smaller, manageable steps.

Set deadlines to keep yourself accountable.

Celebrate progress, no matter how small.

Step 3: Build a Supportive Network

Healing and moving forward are much easier when you're surrounded by people who uplift and encourage you.

Strengthen Existing Relationships

Reconnect with friends and family who have always been there for you.

Plan activities that deepen your bonds, like dinners, trips, or shared hobbies.

Expand Your Social Circle

Join clubs, attend events, or participate in activities that interest you.

Be open to meeting new people, whether through mutual friends, work, or community groups.

Find Role Models

Look for people who inspire you, whether they're friends, public figures, or mentors. Learning from their experiences can provide valuable insight and motivation.

Step 4: Embrace Change

Moving forward often requires stepping out of your comfort zone. While change can be intimidating, it's also where growth happens.

Start with Small Changes

Rearrange your living space to create a fresh environment.

Experiment with a new hairstyle or wardrobe that reflects your current self.

Take Bigger Steps When Ready

Consider moving to a new city or starting a new job.

Pursue a dream you've been putting off, like traveling, starting a business, or going back to school.

Example: After his breakup, Alex decided to fulfill his lifelong dream of backpacking through Europe. The journey not only helped him heal but also gave him a renewed sense of purpose and confidence.

Step 5: Practice Self-Compassion

Moving forward doesn't mean you'll never feel sadness or regret. It's important to treat yourself with kindness during moments of vulnerability.

Forgive Yourself

Let go of guilt or self-blame. Remember that relationships involve two people, and it's rarely one-sided.

Accept that you did your best with the knowledge and resources you had at the time.

Celebrate Your Progress

Reflect on how far you've come since the breakup.

Recognize the inner strength you've developed along the way.

Step 6: Create a Vision for the Future

While the past is behind you, the future is a blank canvas. Take time to imagine what you want your life to look like and start painting that picture.

Visualize Your Ideal Life

What does a typical day look like in your future?

Who are you spending time with, and what are you doing?

Focus on Personal Growth

Pursue opportunities that challenge and inspire you.

Commit to continuous learning, whether through books, courses, or new experiences.

Stay Open to Love

While healing comes first, staying open to the possibility of love in the future can be a beautiful act of hope. When the time is right, you'll be ready to welcome it with a stronger sense of self.

Key Takeaways

Moving forward is about focusing on the present and embracing the possibilities of the future.

Rediscover joy through small moments and meaningful activities.

Set new life goals that align with your values and passions.

Build a supportive network and stay open to positive changes.

Embrace the journey of healing and growth, knowing that brighter days are ahead.

As you close the chapter on this breakup, you're stepping into a new phase of your life—one filled with potential, purpose, and hope. The best is yet to come, and you are more than ready to embrace it.

Reference and Additional Resources

Navigating a breakup and rebuilding your life is a deeply personal journey, but you don't have to do it alone. Below is a list of books, websites, apps, and organizations that can support you in areas such as emotional healing, personal growth, and relationships.

Books

"Rising Strong" by Brené Brown

Explore how vulnerability and resilience can help you overcome setbacks and find strength in the face of heartbreak.

"Attached" by Dr. Amir Levine and Rachel Heller

Gain insights into attachment styles and how they affect your relationships.

"The Gifts of Imperfection" by Brené Brown

Learn to embrace your authenticity and practice self-compassion.

"Letting Go: The Pathway of Surrender" by David R. Hawkins

A practical guide to releasing negative emotions and moving forward.

"Tiny Beautiful Things" by Cheryl Strayed

A collection of heartfelt advice for anyone dealing with life's challenges, including love and loss.

Websites and Online Communities

Psychology Today (**www.psychologytoday.com**[1])

Find articles on emotional well-being and relationships, or search for a therapist near you.

Breakup Recovery (**www.breakuprecovery.net**[2])

Offers practical tips, resources, and community support for healing after a breakup.

Reddit: r/BreakUps

A supportive online community where people share experiences and advice about moving on.

Mind (**www.mind.org.uk**[3])

A UK-based mental health charity with resources for managing emotions and building resilience.

Action for Happiness (**www.actionforhappiness.org**[4])

A site focused on mental well-being and creating positive habits to improve your life.

---

1. **http://www.psychologytoday.com**
2. **http://www.breakuprecovery.net**
3. **http://www.mind.org.uk**
4. **http://www.actionforhappiness.org**

Apps

Headspace

Meditation and mindfulness exercises to help you manage stress and find calm.

Calm

Sleep stories, breathing exercises, and mindfulness techniques for emotional balance.

Mend

An app specifically designed for breakup recovery, with daily lessons and advice.

BetterHelp

An app that connects you to licensed therapists for online counseling.

Moodfit

Track your emotions, set goals, and build habits to improve your mental health.

Therapy and Counseling Resources

Relate (**www.relate.org.uk**[5])

A UK-based organization offering counseling for individuals and couples, including post-breakup support.

Samaritans (**www.samaritans.org**[6])

A 24/7 helpline providing emotional support to anyone in distress (UK: Call 116 123).

National Domestic Abuse Helpline (**www.nationaldahelpline.org.uk**[7])

Support for those leaving abusive relationships. Call 0808 2000 247 (UK).

Counseling Directory (**www.counselling-directory.org.uk**[8])

Search for licensed therapists near you for in-person or online counseling.

WORKSHOPS AND COURSES

The School of Life (**www.theschooloflife.com**[9])

Offers workshops and classes on emotional intelligence, relationships, and personal growth.

Mindfulness-Based Stress Reduction (MBSR)

Explore courses in mindfulness and meditation to help manage emotions and reduce stress.

Meetup (**www.meetup.com**[10])

---

5. **http://www.relate.org.uk**
6. **http://www.samaritans.org**
7. **http://www.nationaldahelpline.org.uk**
8. **http://www.counselling-directory.org.uk**
9. **http://www.theschooloflife.com**

Join local groups focused on personal development, hobbies, or socializing.

10. **http://www.meetup.com**

Podcasts

"Where Should We Begin?" with Esther Perel

A fascinating look into real-life relationship dynamics and healing.

"The Breakup Boost"

Practical advice and motivation for overcoming heartbreak.

"Unlocking Us" by Brené Brown

Episodes on vulnerability, resilience, and personal growth.

"On Purpose with Jay Shetty"

Insightful conversations about mindfulness, relationships, and living intentionally.

Support Groups

Breakup Recovery Support Groups (via Meetup or local organizations)

Join a community of people who understand what you're going through and can offer encouragement.

GriefShare (**www.griefshare.org**[11])

While primarily focused on loss through death, many of their programs include discussions about loss and emotional recovery.

Online Forums: Websites like Better After 50 or specific Reddit communities (e.g., r/ExNoContact) provide peer support.

Inspirational Quotes and Affirmations

If you're seeking daily inspiration, these platforms can be uplifting:

Pinterest: Search for breakup recovery quotes and affirmations.

Instagram Accounts: @WeTheUrban, @TheGoodQuote, or @TherapyForWomen.

---

11. **http://www.griefshare.org**

Practical Tools

Budgeting Tools: If your breakup involves financial changes, apps like You Need a Budget (YNAB) can help you regain control.

Vision Board Apps: Use apps like Canva to create a digital vision board for your goals and aspirations.

Mood Tracking: Apps like Daylio help you monitor your emotional progress over time.

Self-Care Resources

Explore guided yoga or exercise videos on YouTube for stress relief.

Create a playlist of uplifting music to boost your mood.

Dive into creative outlets like coloring books, writing, or crafting.

By exploring these resources, you can continue your journey of healing and self-discovery with the support, inspiration, and tools you need to thrive. Remember, moving forward is about progress, not perfection—and you're not alone in the process.

www.ingramcontent.com/pod-product-compliance
Lightning Source LLC
LaVergne TN
LVHW010116170826
845678LV00012B/2434

* 9 7 9 8 2 3 0 2 3 7 5 0 1 *